50 Delicious Restaurant Noodle Dishes

By: Kelly Johnson

Table of Contents

- Pad Thai
- Spaghetti Carbonara
- Beef Pho
- Ramen
- Yakisoba
- Lo Mein
- Shrimp Scampi
- Fettuccine Alfredo
- Udon
- Dan Dan Noodles
- Bánh Canh
- Soba Noodles
- Pad See Ew
- Singapore Noodles
- Tom Yum Noodles
- Chicken Lo Mein
- Spaghetti Bolognese

- Chicken Pho
- Pesto Pasta
- Hokkien Mee
- Lasagna
- Nasi Goreng
- Spicy Sichuan Noodles
- Noodle Soup with Bok Choy
- Fideuà
- Black Bean Noodles
- Beef Chow Fun
- Shrimp and Grits Noodles
- Chow Mein
- Ziti with Meatballs
- Thai Green Curry Noodles
- Egg Noodles with Garlic Sauce
- Laksa
- Beef Noodle Soup
- Spaghetti with Clams
- Ramen with Soft-Boiled Egg

- Tantanmen
- Cold Noodles with Sesame Sauce
- Gnocchi with Brown Butter Sage
- Kimchi Noodles
- Shoyu Ramen
- Garlic Butter Shrimp Pasta
- Chicken Noodle Soup
- Veggie Stir-Fry Noodles
- Seafood Noodles
- Carbonara Noodles
- Pad Woon Sen
- Tonkotsu Ramen
- Pho Ga
- Chicken and Mushroom Pasta

Pad Thai

Ingredients:

- 8 oz rice noodles
- 2 tbsp vegetable oil
- 1/2 lb shrimp or chicken, diced
- 2 eggs, beaten
- 1/4 cup chopped green onions
- 1/4 cup crushed peanuts
- 2 tbsp fish sauce
- 2 tbsp soy sauce
- 1 tbsp brown sugar
- 1 tbsp lime juice
- 1/2 tsp chili flakes (optional)
- Fresh cilantro, for garnish

Instructions:

1. Cook the rice noodles according to the package instructions. Drain and set aside.
2. In a large pan, heat vegetable oil over medium heat. Add the shrimp or chicken and cook until fully cooked.
3. Push the shrimp or chicken to one side, and add the beaten eggs to the other side of the pan. Scramble the eggs and then mix with the shrimp or chicken.

4. Add the cooked noodles, green onions, fish sauce, soy sauce, brown sugar, lime juice, and chili flakes. Toss to combine and cook for 2-3 minutes until everything is heated through.

5. Garnish with crushed peanuts and cilantro. Serve with lime wedges.

Spaghetti Carbonara

Ingredients:

- 12 oz spaghetti
- 4 oz pancetta or guanciale, diced
- 2 large eggs
- 1/2 cup grated Parmesan cheese
- 1/2 cup grated Pecorino Romano cheese
- 2 cloves garlic, minced
- Salt and pepper, to taste
- Fresh parsley, for garnish

Instructions:

1. Cook the spaghetti in salted water according to the package directions. Drain, reserving some pasta water.
2. In a large pan, cook pancetta or guanciale over medium heat until crispy. Add the minced garlic and cook for 1 minute.
3. In a bowl, whisk together eggs, Parmesan, Pecorino, salt, and pepper.
4. Add the drained spaghetti to the pan with pancetta. Remove from heat and toss to coat. Add the egg mixture and some reserved pasta water to create a creamy sauce.
5. Serve immediately, garnished with parsley and extra cheese.

Beef Pho

Ingredients:

- 1 lb beef sirloin, thinly sliced
- 4 cups beef broth
- 1 onion, halved
- 1 cinnamon stick
- 2-3 star anise
- 4 cloves
- 2 tbsp fish sauce
- 1 tbsp soy sauce
- 1 tbsp sugar
- 1 package rice noodles
- Fresh basil, cilantro, and lime wedges, for garnish
- Sriracha and hoisin sauce, for serving

Instructions:

1. In a large pot, bring the beef broth to a simmer. Add onion, cinnamon stick, star anise, cloves, fish sauce, soy sauce, and sugar. Simmer for 30 minutes, then strain to remove the solids.

2. Cook the rice noodles according to the package instructions. Drain and divide among serving bowls.

3. Pour the hot broth over the noodles, then top with thinly sliced beef. The heat of the broth will cook the beef.

4. Garnish with fresh basil, cilantro, lime wedges, and serve with Sriracha and hoisin sauce.

Ramen

Ingredients:

- 4 cups chicken or pork broth
- 2 cups water
- 2 packs instant ramen noodles (discard the seasoning packet)
- 1 tbsp soy sauce
- 1 tbsp miso paste
- 2 boiled eggs, halved
- 1/2 cup sliced green onions
- 1/2 cup sliced mushrooms
- 1/2 cup cooked chicken or pork (optional)
- 1 tbsp sesame oil

Instructions:

1. In a pot, bring the chicken or pork broth and water to a simmer. Add soy sauce, miso paste, and sesame oil.
2. Cook the ramen noodles in the broth for 3-4 minutes, stirring occasionally.
3. Once the noodles are cooked, divide them among bowls and pour the broth over the noodles.
4. Top with boiled eggs, green onions, mushrooms, and any additional protein (chicken or pork). Serve immediately.

Yakisoba

Ingredients:

- 8 oz yakisoba noodles
- 1 tbsp vegetable oil
- 1/2 lb chicken, thinly sliced
- 1/2 cup sliced cabbage
- 1/2 cup carrots, julienned
- 1/4 cup soy sauce
- 1 tbsp Worcestershire sauce
- 1 tbsp oyster sauce
- 1 tsp sugar
- 1/2 tsp sesame oil
- 1 tbsp sesame seeds (optional)

Instructions:

1. Cook yakisoba noodles according to package instructions and set aside.
2. In a large pan, heat oil over medium heat. Add chicken and cook until browned.
3. Add cabbage and carrots, and stir-fry for another 3-4 minutes.
4. Add the cooked noodles to the pan, followed by soy sauce, Worcestershire sauce, oyster sauce, sugar, and sesame oil. Toss to coat evenly.
5. Garnish with sesame seeds and serve.

Lo Mein

Ingredients:

- 8 oz lo mein noodles
- 1 tbsp vegetable oil
- 1/2 lb shrimp or chicken, diced
- 1 bell pepper, sliced
- 1 carrot, julienned
- 1/2 cup snap peas
- 2 tbsp soy sauce
- 2 tbsp hoisin sauce
- 1 tbsp oyster sauce
- 1/2 tsp sesame oil

Instructions:

1. Cook the lo mein noodles according to the package directions and drain.
2. In a pan, heat oil over medium heat. Add shrimp or chicken and cook until browned.
3. Add the vegetables and stir-fry for 3-4 minutes until tender.
4. Add the cooked noodles to the pan with soy sauce, hoisin sauce, oyster sauce, and sesame oil. Toss everything to combine and cook for an additional 2 minutes.
5. Serve immediately.

Shrimp Scampi

Ingredients:

- 8 oz spaghetti
- 1 lb shrimp, peeled and deveined
- 4 cloves garlic, minced
- 1/4 cup white wine
- 1/4 cup lemon juice
- 1/2 tsp red pepper flakes
- 1/4 cup fresh parsley, chopped
- 1/4 cup Parmesan cheese, grated
- 2 tbsp butter
- Salt and pepper, to taste

Instructions:

1. Cook the spaghetti in salted water according to package directions. Drain, reserving some pasta water.
2. In a large pan, melt butter over medium heat. Add garlic and cook for 1-2 minutes until fragrant.
3. Add the shrimp, white wine, lemon juice, and red pepper flakes. Cook until shrimp are pink and cooked through.
4. Toss the cooked pasta in the pan with the shrimp and sauce, adding reserved pasta water if needed.

5. Garnish with fresh parsley, Parmesan, and serve.

Fettuccine Alfredo

Ingredients:

- 12 oz fettuccine pasta
- 1/2 cup unsalted butter
- 2 cloves garlic, minced
- 1 cup heavy cream
- 1 cup grated Parmesan cheese
- Salt and pepper, to taste
- Fresh parsley, for garnish

Instructions:

1. Cook the fettuccine pasta in salted water according to package directions. Drain.
2. In a pan, melt butter over medium heat. Add garlic and cook until fragrant.
3. Add the heavy cream and simmer for 3-4 minutes. Stir in Parmesan cheese and cook until the sauce thickens.
4. Toss the cooked fettuccine in the sauce, and season with salt and pepper.
5. Garnish with fresh parsley and serve.

Udon

Ingredients:

- 8 oz udon noodles
- 4 cups dashi broth
- 2 tbsp soy sauce
- 1 tbsp mirin
- 1/4 cup sliced green onions
- 1/2 cup sliced mushrooms
- 1/4 cup nori (seaweed), for garnish
- 1 boiled egg, halved (optional)

Instructions:

1. Cook the udon noodles according to the package directions. Drain.
2. In a pot, bring the dashi broth to a simmer. Add soy sauce and mirin.
3. Add the cooked noodles to the pot and heat through.
4. Serve the udon in bowls, topped with green onions, mushrooms, nori, and a boiled egg (if desired).

Dan Dan Noodles

Ingredients:

- 8 oz Chinese wheat noodles
- 2 tbsp sesame paste
- 2 tbsp soy sauce
- 1 tbsp rice vinegar
- 1 tbsp chili oil
- 1/2 tsp Sichuan peppercorns (optional)
- 1/2 lb ground pork
- 2 cloves garlic, minced
- 2 tbsp green onions, chopped
- 1/4 cup peanuts, crushed
- 1/4 cup pickled mustard greens (optional)

Instructions:

1. Cook the Chinese wheat noodles according to the package directions. Drain and set aside.
2. In a bowl, whisk together sesame paste, soy sauce, rice vinegar, chili oil, and Sichuan peppercorns.
3. In a pan, cook ground pork with minced garlic over medium heat until browned.
4. To serve, place noodles in a bowl, top with the pork mixture, then drizzle with the sesame sauce.
5. Garnish with green onions, crushed peanuts, and pickled mustard greens.

Bánh Canh

Ingredients:

- 8 oz bánh canh noodles (thick Vietnamese tapioca noodles)
- 1 lb pork or shrimp (or a mix), diced
- 4 cups chicken or pork broth
- 2 tbsp fish sauce
- 1 tbsp soy sauce
- 1 tsp sugar
- 1/2 onion, sliced
- 2 cloves garlic, minced
- Fresh cilantro, for garnish
- Lime wedges, for serving
- Sliced chili peppers (optional)

Instructions:

1. Cook the bánh canh noodles in boiling water according to package directions. Drain and set aside.
2. In a pot, sauté onions and garlic in oil until fragrant.
3. Add the pork or shrimp and cook until browned.
4. Add the broth, fish sauce, soy sauce, and sugar. Bring to a boil, then reduce to a simmer for 15-20 minutes.
5. To serve, divide the noodles into bowls and ladle the broth and meat mixture over them.
6. Garnish with cilantro, lime wedges, and chili peppers.

Soba Noodles

Ingredients:

- 8 oz soba noodles
- 2 tbsp soy sauce
- 2 tbsp mirin
- 1 tbsp sesame oil
- 1 tsp rice vinegar
- 1 tbsp green onions, chopped
- 1 tbsp sesame seeds
- 1 boiled egg, halved (optional)

Instructions:

1. Cook the soba noodles in boiling water according to package instructions. Drain and rinse under cold water to stop cooking.
2. In a bowl, mix soy sauce, mirin, sesame oil, and rice vinegar.
3. Toss the cooked noodles with the sauce mixture.
4. Garnish with green onions, sesame seeds, and a boiled egg (optional).

Pad See Ew

Ingredients:

- 8 oz wide rice noodles
- 2 tbsp vegetable oil
- 1/2 lb chicken or pork, sliced
- 1 egg, beaten
- 1 cup Chinese broccoli (gai lan) or regular broccoli, chopped
- 2 tbsp soy sauce
- 1 tbsp dark soy sauce
- 1 tbsp oyster sauce
- 1 tbsp sugar
- 1/4 tsp white pepper

Instructions:

1. Cook the rice noodles according to the package instructions. Drain and set aside.
2. In a large pan or wok, heat the vegetable oil over medium heat. Add the sliced chicken or pork and cook until browned.
3. Add the beaten egg and scramble until fully cooked.
4. Add the Chinese broccoli and cook for 2-3 minutes.
5. Add the cooked noodles, soy sauce, dark soy sauce, oyster sauce, sugar, and white pepper. Toss to combine and cook for another 2-3 minutes.
6. Serve immediately.

Singapore Noodles

Ingredients:

- 8 oz rice vermicelli noodles
- 2 tbsp vegetable oil
- 1/2 lb shrimp, peeled and deveined
- 1/2 bell pepper, julienned
- 1/2 onion, sliced
- 1/2 cup snow peas
- 2 cloves garlic, minced
- 2 tbsp curry powder
- 2 tbsp soy sauce
- 1 tbsp oyster sauce
- 1 tbsp sesame oil
- Fresh cilantro, for garnish

Instructions:

1. Cook the rice vermicelli noodles according to package instructions. Drain and set aside.
2. In a large pan, heat vegetable oil over medium heat. Add shrimp and cook until pink.
3. Add the bell pepper, onion, and snow peas, and sauté for 3-4 minutes.
4. Add garlic and curry powder, stirring for another minute.
5. Add the cooked noodles, soy sauce, oyster sauce, and sesame oil. Toss to combine and heat through.
6. Garnish with fresh cilantro and serve.

Tom Yum Noodles

Ingredients:

- 8 oz rice noodles
- 4 cups chicken broth
- 1 stalk lemongrass, smashed
- 3-4 kaffir lime leaves
- 2-3 Thai bird's eye chilies, smashed
- 2 tbsp fish sauce
- 1 tbsp lime juice
- 1 tsp sugar
- 1/2 lb shrimp, peeled and deveined
- Fresh cilantro, for garnish

Instructions:

1. Cook the rice noodles according to the package instructions. Drain and set aside.
2. In a pot, bring the chicken broth to a boil. Add lemongrass, kaffir lime leaves, and bird's eye chilies. Simmer for 10-15 minutes.
3. Add fish sauce, lime juice, and sugar.
4. Add the shrimp and cook for 3-4 minutes until pink.
5. To serve, divide the noodles into bowls and pour the broth and shrimp mixture over them.
6. Garnish with fresh cilantro.

Chicken Lo Mein

Ingredients:

- 8 oz lo mein noodles
- 2 tbsp vegetable oil
- 1 lb chicken breast, thinly sliced
- 1/2 onion, sliced
- 1 bell pepper, sliced
- 1 carrot, julienned
- 2 tbsp soy sauce
- 1 tbsp oyster sauce
- 1 tbsp hoisin sauce
- 1 tsp sesame oil

Instructions:

1. Cook the lo mein noodles according to package instructions. Drain and set aside.
2. In a large pan, heat vegetable oil over medium heat. Add chicken and cook until browned.
3. Add the onion, bell pepper, and carrot, and sauté until softened.
4. Add the cooked noodles and toss to combine.
5. Add soy sauce, oyster sauce, hoisin sauce, and sesame oil, and stir until well combined.
6. Serve immediately.

Spaghetti Bolognese

Ingredients:

- 12 oz spaghetti
- 1 lb ground beef or pork
- 1 onion, chopped
- 2 cloves garlic, minced
- 1 can (14 oz) crushed tomatoes
- 1/4 cup red wine (optional)
- 1 tbsp Italian seasoning
- 1/2 cup milk or cream
- Salt and pepper, to taste
- Fresh basil, for garnish
- Grated Parmesan cheese, for garnish

Instructions:

1. Cook the spaghetti according to package directions. Drain and set aside.
2. In a large pan, cook ground meat with onion and garlic until browned.
3. Add crushed tomatoes, red wine (if using), Italian seasoning, salt, and pepper. Simmer for 20-30 minutes.
4. Stir in milk or cream and simmer for another 5 minutes.
5. Serve the sauce over the spaghetti, garnished with fresh basil and Parmesan cheese.

Chicken Pho

Ingredients:

- 8 oz rice noodles
- 4 cups chicken broth
- 1 onion, halved
- 2-3 slices ginger
- 2 tbsp fish sauce
- 1 tbsp soy sauce
- 1 tbsp sugar
- 1/2 lb chicken breast, thinly sliced
- Fresh basil, cilantro, lime wedges, and sliced chili peppers, for garnish

Instructions:

1. Cook the rice noodles according to package directions. Drain and set aside.
2. In a pot, bring chicken broth to a boil. Add onion, ginger, fish sauce, soy sauce, and sugar. Simmer for 15-20 minutes.
3. Add the sliced chicken and cook until just cooked through.
4. Serve the noodles in bowls and pour the broth over the top.
5. Garnish with fresh basil, cilantro, lime wedges, and chili peppers.

Pesto Pasta

Ingredients:

- 12 oz pasta (spaghetti, fusilli, or penne)
- 1 cup fresh basil leaves
- 1/4 cup pine nuts (or walnuts)
- 2 cloves garlic
- 1/2 cup extra virgin olive oil
- 1/4 cup grated Parmesan cheese
- Salt and pepper, to taste

Instructions:

1. Cook pasta according to package instructions. Drain and set aside, reserving some pasta water.
2. In a food processor, blend basil, pine nuts, garlic, olive oil, and Parmesan until smooth.
3. Toss the pesto sauce with the cooked pasta, adding a little reserved pasta water if needed for consistency.
4. Season with salt and pepper to taste, and serve.

Hokkien Mee

Ingredients:

- 8 oz Hokkien noodles or egg noodles
- 1/2 lb shrimp, peeled and deveined
- 1/2 lb pork belly or chicken, thinly sliced
- 2 tbsp vegetable oil
- 1 onion, sliced
- 2 cloves garlic, minced
- 2 cups chicken broth
- 2 tbsp soy sauce
- 1 tbsp oyster sauce
- 1/2 tsp white pepper
- 2 eggs, beaten
- 2 green onions, chopped
- Lime wedges for serving

Instructions:

1. Cook Hokkien noodles according to package instructions. Drain and set aside.
2. In a wok, heat vegetable oil over medium heat. Add shrimp and pork belly/chicken and cook until browned. Remove from the wok.
3. Add onion and garlic to the wok and cook until fragrant. Add the broth, soy sauce, oyster sauce, and white pepper. Bring to a boil.
4. Add the cooked noodles to the broth and toss to combine. Push noodles to the side, pour in beaten eggs, and scramble until cooked.

5. Return shrimp and pork/chicken to the wok and stir everything together.

6. Garnish with green onions and serve with lime wedges.

Lasagna

Ingredients:

- 12 oz lasagna noodles
- 1 lb ground beef or pork
- 1 onion, chopped
- 2 cloves garlic, minced
- 1 can (14 oz) crushed tomatoes
- 1 can (6 oz) tomato paste
- 2 tbsp tomato sauce
- 1/4 cup fresh basil, chopped
- 1/4 cup parsley, chopped
- 2 cups ricotta cheese
- 3 cups mozzarella cheese, shredded
- 1/2 cup Parmesan cheese, grated
- Salt and pepper, to taste

Instructions:

1. Preheat oven to 375°F (190°C). Cook lasagna noodles according to package instructions. Drain and set aside.

2. In a pan, cook ground beef, onion, and garlic until browned. Add crushed tomatoes, tomato paste, tomato sauce, basil, parsley, salt, and pepper. Simmer for 20-30 minutes.

3. In a separate bowl, mix ricotta cheese with half of the mozzarella and Parmesan.

4. In a baking dish, layer noodles, meat sauce, and cheese mixture. Repeat until all ingredients are used, finishing with a layer of mozzarella cheese.

5. Bake for 25-30 minutes, until the cheese is bubbly and golden. Let cool for 10 minutes before serving.

Nasi Goreng

Ingredients:

- 2 cups cooked rice (preferably cold)
- 2 tbsp vegetable oil
- 2 cloves garlic, minced
- 1/2 onion, chopped
- 1/2 cup cooked chicken or shrimp, chopped
- 2 eggs, beaten
- 2 tbsp soy sauce
- 1 tbsp oyster sauce
- 1 tsp sugar
- 1/2 tsp chili paste (optional)
- 2 green onions, chopped
- Cucumber and tomato slices, for garnish

Instructions:

1. Heat vegetable oil in a large pan or wok. Add garlic and onion and sauté until fragrant.
2. Add chicken or shrimp and cook for 2-3 minutes.
3. Push the mixture to the side of the pan and scramble the eggs in the same pan.
4. Add the rice, soy sauce, oyster sauce, sugar, and chili paste. Stir well to combine.
5. Stir in green onions and serve with cucumber and tomato slices.

Spicy Sichuan Noodles

Ingredients:

- 8 oz noodles (egg noodles or spaghetti)
- 2 tbsp vegetable oil
- 2 cloves garlic, minced
- 1 tbsp ginger, minced
- 2 tbsp Sichuan peppercorns
- 3 tbsp soy sauce
- 1 tbsp rice vinegar
- 1 tbsp chili paste or chili oil
- 1 tbsp sugar
- 1 tbsp sesame oil
- 1 tbsp peanut butter (optional)
- Green onions, chopped, for garnish

Instructions:

1. Cook noodles according to package instructions. Drain and set aside.
2. In a wok, heat vegetable oil and add garlic, ginger, and Sichuan peppercorns. Cook until fragrant.
3. Add soy sauce, rice vinegar, chili paste, sugar, sesame oil, and peanut butter. Stir to combine.
4. Add cooked noodles to the wok and toss to coat with the sauce.
5. Garnish with green onions and serve.

Noodle Soup with Bok Choy

Ingredients:

- 8 oz noodles (egg noodles or ramen)
- 4 cups chicken or vegetable broth
- 1 tbsp soy sauce
- 1 tbsp sesame oil
- 2 cloves garlic, minced
- 1/2 onion, sliced
- 1 bunch bok choy, chopped
- 1/2 cup mushrooms, sliced
- 1 tbsp green onions, chopped
- Soft-boiled egg (optional)

Instructions:

1. Cook the noodles according to package instructions. Drain and set aside.
2. In a pot, bring the broth to a boil. Add soy sauce, sesame oil, garlic, onion, bok choy, and mushrooms. Simmer for 5-7 minutes.
3. Divide cooked noodles into bowls and pour the soup over the top.
4. Garnish with green onions and a soft-boiled egg if desired.

Fideuà

Ingredients:

- 8 oz fideuà noodles (short, thin noodles)
- 1/2 lb seafood (shrimp, mussels, squid)
- 1/2 lb chicken, diced
- 1 onion, chopped
- 2 cloves garlic, minced
- 2 tomatoes, grated
- 2 cups chicken broth
- 1/4 cup white wine
- 1/2 tsp saffron threads
- 1/4 cup parsley, chopped
- Lemon wedges for serving

Instructions:

1. In a paella pan or large skillet, sauté chicken, onion, and garlic in olive oil until browned.
2. Add seafood and cook until just done.
3. Add grated tomatoes, white wine, and saffron. Stir for 1-2 minutes.
4. Pour in the chicken broth and bring to a boil. Add the fideuà noodles and cook until tender, about 10-12 minutes.
5. Garnish with parsley and serve with lemon wedges.

Black Bean Noodles

Ingredients:

- 8 oz noodles (ramen or soba)
- 2 tbsp vegetable oil
- 1/2 onion, sliced
- 2 cloves garlic, minced
- 1/2 cup black beans, drained and rinsed
- 2 tbsp soy sauce
- 1 tbsp oyster sauce
- 1 tbsp sugar
- 1 tbsp sesame oil
- 1/2 tsp chili flakes (optional)
- Green onions, chopped, for garnish

Instructions:

1. Cook the noodles according to package instructions. Drain and set aside.
2. In a pan, heat vegetable oil and sauté onion and garlic until fragrant.
3. Add black beans, soy sauce, oyster sauce, sugar, sesame oil, and chili flakes. Stir well.
4. Add the cooked noodles and toss to combine.
5. Garnish with green onions and serve.

Beef Chow Fun

Ingredients:

- 8 oz wide rice noodles
- 1 lb flank steak, thinly sliced
- 2 tbsp soy sauce
- 2 tbsp oyster sauce
- 1 tbsp soy sauce
- 1 tbsp sugar
- 2 tbsp vegetable oil
- 1/2 onion, sliced
- 1/2 bell pepper, sliced
- 2 cloves garlic, minced
- Green onions, chopped, for garnish

Instructions:

1. Cook the rice noodles according to package instructions. Drain and set aside.
2. Marinate the beef slices in 1 tbsp soy sauce, 1 tbsp oyster sauce, and sugar.
3. Heat vegetable oil in a wok and cook beef until browned. Remove from the wok.
4. Add onion, bell pepper, and garlic to the wok and sauté until softened.
5. Add the cooked noodles and toss to combine.
6. Return the beef to the wok, add soy sauce, and oyster sauce, and stir everything together.
7. Garnish with green onions and serve.

Shrimp and Grits Noodles

Ingredients:

- 8 oz pasta (linguine or spaghetti)
- 1 lb shrimp, peeled and deveined
- 1 cup grits (or polenta)
- 2 cups water or chicken broth
- 1 tbsp butter
- 2 cloves garlic, minced
- 1/4 cup Parmesan cheese
- 1 tbsp lemon juice
- Salt and pepper to taste
- Green onions, chopped, for garnish

Instructions:

1. Cook the pasta according to package instructions. Drain and set aside.
2. In a pot, bring water or chicken broth to a boil and cook grits according to package instructions.
3. In a skillet, melt butter and sauté garlic until fragrant. Add shrimp and cook until pink.
4. Add cooked grits, Parmesan, and lemon juice to the shrimp. Stir to combine.
5. Serve the shrimp and grits mixture over pasta, garnished with green onions.

Chow Mein

Ingredients:

- 8 oz chow mein noodles
- 1 tbsp vegetable oil
- 1 onion, sliced
- 2 cloves garlic, minced
- 1 carrot, julienned
- 1 bell pepper, sliced
- 1/2 cup cabbage, shredded
- 2 tbsp soy sauce
- 1 tbsp oyster sauce
- 1 tbsp hoisin sauce
- 1 tsp sesame oil
- 1 tbsp green onions, chopped

Instructions:

1. Cook chow mein noodles according to package instructions. Drain and set aside.
2. Heat vegetable oil in a wok over medium heat. Add onion, garlic, carrot, bell pepper, and cabbage. Stir-fry until vegetables are tender.
3. Add the cooked noodles and stir to combine.
4. Add soy sauce, oyster sauce, hoisin sauce, and sesame oil. Toss well and cook for another 2 minutes.
5. Garnish with green onions and serve.

Ziti with Meatballs

Ingredients:

- 12 oz ziti pasta
- 1 lb ground beef or pork
- 1/2 cup breadcrumbs
- 1/4 cup grated Parmesan cheese
- 1 egg
- 2 cloves garlic, minced
- 1 tbsp parsley, chopped
- 2 cups marinara sauce
- Salt and pepper, to taste

Instructions:

1. Preheat the oven to 375°F (190°C).
2. In a bowl, combine ground meat, breadcrumbs, Parmesan, egg, garlic, parsley, salt, and pepper. Shape into meatballs.
3. Place meatballs on a baking sheet and bake for 20-25 minutes, or until browned.
4. While the meatballs bake, cook the ziti according to package instructions. Drain and set aside.
5. In a pan, heat marinara sauce. Add the meatballs and simmer for 10 minutes.
6. Toss cooked ziti with sauce and meatballs. Serve hot.

Thai Green Curry Noodles

Ingredients:

- 8 oz rice noodles
- 1 tbsp vegetable oil
- 1 onion, chopped
- 1 bell pepper, sliced
- 2 tbsp green curry paste
- 1 can (14 oz) coconut milk
- 1 tbsp fish sauce
- 1 tbsp sugar
- 1/4 cup basil leaves, chopped
- 1 tbsp lime juice
- Green onions for garnish

Instructions:

1. Cook rice noodles according to package instructions. Drain and set aside.
2. In a pan, heat oil over medium heat. Add onion and bell pepper and sauté until tender.
3. Stir in green curry paste and cook for 1 minute.
4. Add coconut milk, fish sauce, and sugar. Stir and bring to a simmer.
5. Toss in the cooked noodles and basil leaves. Cook for 2 minutes.
6. Remove from heat, add lime juice, and serve garnished with green onions.

Egg Noodles with Garlic Sauce

Ingredients:

- 8 oz egg noodles
- 2 tbsp vegetable oil
- 3 cloves garlic, minced
- 2 tbsp soy sauce
- 1 tbsp oyster sauce
- 1 tbsp sesame oil
- 1/2 tsp sugar
- 1 tbsp green onions, chopped
- Red pepper flakes, optional

Instructions:

1. Cook egg noodles according to package instructions. Drain and set aside.
2. In a pan, heat oil over medium heat. Add garlic and sauté until fragrant.
3. Stir in soy sauce, oyster sauce, sesame oil, and sugar.
4. Add the cooked noodles and toss to coat.
5. Garnish with green onions and red pepper flakes, if desired.

Laksa

Ingredients:

- 8 oz rice noodles
- 1 tbsp vegetable oil
- 1 onion, chopped
- 2 cloves garlic, minced
- 1 tbsp ginger, minced
- 1 tbsp red curry paste
- 1 can (14 oz) coconut milk
- 2 cups chicken broth
- 1 tbsp soy sauce
- 1/2 lb shrimp, peeled and deveined
- 2 boiled eggs, halved
- 1/4 cup cilantro, chopped
- Lime wedges for serving

Instructions:

1. Cook rice noodles according to package instructions. Drain and set aside.
2. In a pot, heat oil over medium heat. Add onion, garlic, and ginger. Sauté until softened.
3. Stir in red curry paste and cook for 1 minute.
4. Add coconut milk, chicken broth, and soy sauce. Bring to a simmer.
5. Add shrimp and cook until pink.

6. Divide noodles into bowls. Pour soup over noodles, top with shrimp, boiled eggs, and cilantro.

7. Serve with lime wedges.

Beef Noodle Soup

Ingredients:

- 8 oz egg noodles
- 2 tbsp vegetable oil
- 1 lb beef (chuck or brisket), sliced
- 2 cloves garlic, minced
- 4 cups beef broth
- 2 tbsp soy sauce
- 1 tbsp hoisin sauce
- 1 tsp five-spice powder
- 1/4 cup green onions, chopped
- 1/4 cup cilantro, chopped
- Lime wedges for serving

Instructions:

1. Cook egg noodles according to package instructions. Drain and set aside.
2. In a pot, heat vegetable oil over medium heat. Add beef and garlic. Cook until beef is browned.
3. Add beef broth, soy sauce, hoisin sauce, and five-spice powder. Bring to a simmer and cook for 30 minutes.
4. Divide cooked noodles into bowls. Pour soup over noodles.
5. Garnish with green onions, cilantro, and lime wedges.

Spaghetti with Clams

Ingredients:

- 8 oz spaghetti
- 2 tbsp olive oil
- 3 cloves garlic, minced
- 1/4 tsp red pepper flakes
- 1 can (10 oz) clams, drained
- 1/2 cup white wine
- 1/4 cup parsley, chopped
- Lemon wedges for serving

Instructions:

1. Cook spaghetti according to package instructions. Drain and set aside.
2. In a pan, heat olive oil over medium heat. Add garlic and red pepper flakes. Sauté for 1 minute.
3. Add clams and white wine. Cook for 3-4 minutes until heated through.
4. Toss in the cooked spaghetti and parsley.
5. Serve with lemon wedges.

Ramen with Soft-Boiled Egg

Ingredients:

- 2 packs ramen noodles
- 4 cups chicken broth
- 2 tbsp soy sauce
- 2 tbsp miso paste
- 1 tbsp sesame oil
- 2 eggs
- 1/2 cup green onions, chopped
- 1/4 cup nori, shredded

Instructions:

1. Bring water to a boil in a pot and carefully lower in eggs. Boil for 7-8 minutes for soft-boiled eggs. Remove and set aside.
2. In a separate pot, bring chicken broth to a simmer. Stir in soy sauce, miso paste, and sesame oil.
3. Cook ramen noodles according to package instructions.
4. Divide noodles into bowls and pour broth over them.
5. Peel and halve the eggs, placing them on top of the ramen. Garnish with green onions and nori.

Tantanmen

Ingredients:

- 8 oz noodles (ramen or udon)
- 2 tbsp sesame paste
- 1 tbsp soy sauce
- 1 tbsp rice vinegar
- 1 tsp chili oil
- 1 tbsp peanut butter
- 1/2 lb ground pork
- 2 cloves garlic, minced
- 1 tbsp ginger, minced
- 1/4 cup green onions, chopped
- 1 tbsp sesame seeds

Instructions:

1. Cook noodles according to package instructions. Drain and set aside.
2. In a pan, cook ground pork with garlic and ginger until browned.
3. In a bowl, combine sesame paste, soy sauce, rice vinegar, chili oil, and peanut butter. Add a little water to reach desired consistency.
4. Toss the cooked noodles with the sesame mixture.
5. Top with the cooked pork, green onions, and sesame seeds.

Cold Noodles with Sesame Sauce

Ingredients:

- 8 oz noodles (soba or egg noodles)
- 2 tbsp sesame paste
- 2 tbsp soy sauce
- 1 tbsp rice vinegar
- 1 tsp sugar
- 1/2 tsp sesame oil
- 1 cucumber, julienned
- 1/4 cup cilantro, chopped
- Crushed peanuts, for garnish

Instructions:

1. Cook noodles according to package instructions. Drain and rinse with cold water.
2. In a bowl, whisk together sesame paste, soy sauce, rice vinegar, sugar, and sesame oil.
3. Toss the noodles with the sesame sauce.
4. Garnish with cucumber, cilantro, and crushed peanuts. Serve chilled.

Gnocchi with Brown Butter Sage

Ingredients:

- 1 lb gnocchi
- 4 tbsp unsalted butter
- 10 fresh sage leaves
- 1/4 cup grated Parmesan cheese
- Salt and pepper, to taste

Instructions:

1. Cook gnocchi according to package instructions. Drain and set aside.
2. In a large pan, melt butter over medium heat. Once melted, add sage leaves and cook until butter turns golden brown and fragrant (about 3 minutes).
3. Add cooked gnocchi to the pan and toss to coat in the brown butter.
4. Season with salt and pepper, then serve topped with grated Parmesan.

Kimchi Noodles

Ingredients:

- 8 oz noodles (ramen or udon)
- 1/2 cup kimchi, chopped
- 1 tbsp vegetable oil
- 2 cloves garlic, minced
- 2 tbsp soy sauce
- 1 tbsp gochujang (Korean chili paste)
- 1 tbsp rice vinegar
- 1 tbsp sesame oil
- 1 tbsp sesame seeds
- 1/4 cup green onions, chopped

Instructions:

1. Cook noodles according to package instructions. Drain and set aside.
2. In a pan, heat vegetable oil over medium heat. Add garlic and sauté until fragrant.
3. Add chopped kimchi and cook for 2-3 minutes.
4. Stir in soy sauce, gochujang, rice vinegar, and sesame oil.
5. Toss in the cooked noodles and mix well.
6. Garnish with sesame seeds and green onions before serving.

Shoyu Ramen

Ingredients:

- 2 packs ramen noodles
- 4 cups chicken or pork broth
- 2 tbsp soy sauce
- 1 tbsp mirin
- 1 tbsp sesame oil
- 1 tsp ginger, grated
- 2 cloves garlic, minced
- 1/4 cup green onions, chopped
- 1/4 cup nori, shredded
- Soft-boiled egg (optional)

Instructions:

1. Cook ramen noodles according to package instructions. Drain and set aside.
2. In a pot, heat sesame oil over medium heat. Add garlic and ginger, sauté until fragrant.
3. Add the broth, soy sauce, and mirin to the pot. Bring to a simmer.
4. Divide cooked noodles into bowls and pour broth over the noodles.
5. Garnish with green onions, nori, and soft-boiled egg, if desired.

Garlic Butter Shrimp Pasta

Ingredients:

- 8 oz pasta (linguine or spaghetti)
- 1 lb shrimp, peeled and deveined
- 4 tbsp butter
- 6 cloves garlic, minced
- 1/2 cup white wine (optional)
- 1/4 cup Parmesan cheese, grated
- Salt and pepper, to taste
- 2 tbsp parsley, chopped

Instructions:

1. Cook pasta according to package instructions. Drain and set aside.
2. In a large skillet, melt butter over medium heat. Add garlic and sauté until fragrant.
3. Add shrimp to the pan and cook until pink, about 3-4 minutes.
4. Add white wine (if using) and cook for another minute.
5. Toss in the cooked pasta and mix until the pasta is coated with the garlic butter.
6. Season with salt and pepper, and top with Parmesan and parsley before serving.

Chicken Noodle Soup

Ingredients:

- 2 tbsp olive oil
- 1 onion, chopped
- 2 carrots, sliced
- 2 celery stalks, chopped
- 2 cloves garlic, minced
- 6 cups chicken broth
- 1 lb chicken breast or thighs, cooked and shredded
- 1 1/2 cups egg noodles
- Salt and pepper, to taste
- 1/4 cup parsley, chopped

Instructions:

1. In a pot, heat olive oil over medium heat. Add onion, carrots, and celery. Cook until softened, about 5-7 minutes.
2. Add garlic and cook for 1 minute.
3. Pour in chicken broth and bring to a boil.
4. Add the shredded chicken and egg noodles. Cook for 10 minutes, until noodles are tender.
5. Season with salt and pepper, and garnish with parsley before serving.

Veggie Stir-Fry Noodles

Ingredients:

- 8 oz noodles (rice noodles or lo mein)
- 1 tbsp vegetable oil
- 1 bell pepper, sliced
- 1 carrot, julienned
- 1 zucchini, sliced
- 1/2 cup snap peas
- 2 tbsp soy sauce
- 1 tbsp hoisin sauce
- 1 tbsp sesame oil
- 1 tbsp sesame seeds
- Green onions, chopped

Instructions:

1. Cook noodles according to package instructions. Drain and set aside.
2. In a pan, heat vegetable oil over medium heat. Add bell pepper, carrot, zucchini, and snap peas. Stir-fry for 5-6 minutes.
3. Stir in soy sauce, hoisin sauce, and sesame oil.
4. Add cooked noodles and toss to combine.
5. Garnish with sesame seeds and green onions before serving.

Seafood Noodles

Ingredients:

- 8 oz noodles (egg noodles or spaghetti)
- 1 tbsp olive oil
- 1/2 lb shrimp, peeled and deveined
- 1/2 lb scallops
- 2 cloves garlic, minced
- 1/4 cup white wine
- 1/4 cup heavy cream
- 1/4 cup Parmesan cheese, grated
- Salt and pepper, to taste
- Fresh parsley, chopped

Instructions:

1. Cook noodles according to package instructions. Drain and set aside.
2. In a large skillet, heat olive oil over medium heat. Add garlic and sauté until fragrant.
3. Add shrimp and scallops to the pan and cook until golden and opaque, about 3-4 minutes per side.
4. Pour in white wine and let it reduce by half.
5. Add heavy cream and Parmesan cheese, stirring to combine.
6. Toss in the cooked noodles and coat with the sauce.
7. Season with salt and pepper, and garnish with fresh parsley before serving.

Carbonara Noodles

Ingredients:

- 8 oz pasta (spaghetti or fettuccine)
- 4 oz pancetta or bacon, diced
- 2 eggs
- 1/2 cup Parmesan cheese, grated
- Salt and pepper, to taste
- 1 tbsp parsley, chopped

Instructions:

1. Cook pasta according to package instructions. Drain, reserving 1/2 cup of pasta water.
2. In a pan, cook pancetta or bacon until crispy, about 5-6 minutes.
3. In a bowl, whisk eggs with Parmesan cheese, salt, and pepper.
4. Add cooked pasta to the pan with pancetta, and toss to combine.
5. Remove from heat and quickly pour the egg mixture over the pasta. Toss well to coat the noodles.
6. Add reserved pasta water to reach desired consistency.
7. Garnish with parsley and serve immediately.

Pad Woon Sen

Ingredients:

- 8 oz glass noodles
- 1 tbsp vegetable oil
- 2 cloves garlic, minced
- 1 egg, beaten
- 1/2 cup carrots, julienned
- 1/2 cup bell peppers, sliced
- 1/4 cup soy sauce
- 1 tbsp fish sauce
- 1 tbsp oyster sauce
- 1 tsp sugar
- 1/4 cup cilantro, chopped
- Lime wedges for serving

Instructions:

1. Cook glass noodles according to package instructions. Drain and set aside.
2. In a pan, heat vegetable oil over medium heat. Add garlic and sauté until fragrant.
3. Push garlic to one side and add the beaten egg to the pan. Scramble the egg until cooked.
4. Add carrots and bell peppers, cooking for 2-3 minutes.
5. Stir in soy sauce, fish sauce, oyster sauce, and sugar.
6. Add the cooked noodles and toss to coat.

7. Garnish with cilantro and serve with lime wedges.

Tonkotsu Ramen

Ingredients:

- 2 packs ramen noodles
- 4 cups pork broth
- 2 tbsp soy sauce
- 1 tbsp miso paste
- 1 tbsp sesame oil
- 1 tsp ginger, grated
- 2 cloves garlic, minced
- 2 eggs (soft-boiled)
- 1/4 cup green onions, chopped
- 1/4 cup nori, shredded

Instructions:

1. Cook ramen noodles according to package instructions. Drain and set aside.
2. In a pot, heat sesame oil over medium heat. Add garlic and ginger, sauté until fragrant.
3. Pour in pork broth, soy sauce, and miso paste. Simmer for 10-15 minutes.
4. Divide cooked noodles into bowls and pour broth over the noodles.
5. Garnish with soft-boiled eggs, green onions, and shredded nori.

Pho Ga

Ingredients:

- 1 lb chicken breast or thighs
- 1 onion, quartered
- 2-inch piece of ginger, sliced
- 2 cloves garlic, smashed
- 2 cinnamon sticks
- 4 star anise
- 4 cups chicken broth
- 1 tbsp fish sauce
- 8 oz rice noodles
- 1/4 cup cilantro, chopped
- 1/4 cup basil, chopped
- Lime wedges
- Bean sprouts

Instructions:

1. In a large pot, add chicken, onion, ginger, garlic, cinnamon sticks, and star anise.
2. Pour in chicken broth and bring to a boil.
3. Reduce heat and simmer for 30 minutes.
4. Remove chicken, shred it, and return it to the pot.
5. Add fish sauce and cook rice noodles according to package instructions.
6. Serve the pho with fresh cilantro, basil, lime wedges, and bean sprouts.

www.ingramcontent.com/pod-product-compliance
Lightning Source LLC
LaVergne TN
LVHW081319060526
838201LV00055B/2367